Uni·

T   R
  I   E
    M   T
      E   T
          *   A
            M
        BECOMING
            Y
          G   S
        R   P
      E   A
    N   C
E   E

Collected Poems of

Robert Charles Howard

Poems written by Robert Charles Howard between the years of 2004 and 2015.

ISBN-13: 978-1514894439

Cover photos and design by Robin Howard

Preface:

In the spring of 2004 I was commissioned to compose a cantata in commemoration of the bicentennial of the Lewis and Clark expedition for the Belleville Philharmonic and was in dire need of a text. I asked several literary friends to come on board but finding no takers I had no choice but to draft myself.

After a solid year of work, the ship was launched and I was left with a full head of creative steam and needing a way to wind down, I turned to writing poems and haven't stopped since.

I am very fond of having new experiences and seeing new places so the poems you have before you reflect my curiosity about the natural world and the complexities of our human family. In defiance of the obvious physical constraints, I am also hooked on time and space travel, so prepare yourself for a few wild and strange rides.

Some of the poems such as Living Brahms, Beethoven's Walk and Pictures at an Exhibition reflect my "other life" as a conductor and composer and are poetic responses to performances I have led.

Three of the poems, Song of the Rockies, Alpenglow and Canticle of Hope were written as part of my cantata for the centennial of Rocky Mountain National Park called Wilderness Reflections (most of the texts for that work are poems by Wendell Berry).

I am very grateful for my poetic mentors, professors, Gordon Jackson and William F. Dougherty for their critical reading of my early attempts and for holding no prisoners.

Special thanks to Dr. Kathryn Bowers for asking me to write "Wilderness Reflections" and to all the fine musicians who sang or played in the premier under the able leadership of Kathryn Bowers.

I am also grateful for the lovely cover that my wife, Robin designed for this book and for my many friends of the Belleville Philharmonic Orchestra and Chorale for inspiring me with the pure poetry of their playing and singing.

Table of Contents

Part I – Our Island Home

Part II – Music of the Spheres

Part III – Human Family Picnic

Part IV – Ancient Footprints

Part V – A Place to Call Home

PART I – OUR ISLAND HOME

Landscapes

If I had a flying carpet,
I'd fly you to the falls
to watch the rainbows shimmer
in the rock-spewn mists
of Niagra's reckless plunge.

Or share the blazing sunset
at Big Bend's mystic window:
gazing at pastel layers
merged with the western sky.

Or we'd lower a canoe
in a Missouri stream
on a star-jeweled moonlit night
and hear the dulcet songs
of gentle shore-bound waves
and the hum of an insect choir.

But I have no magic carpet
to whisk you off to peaceful vistas:
only these feeble runes
scratched on a field of white.

Still, I wish that we could get away -
that is -
if you can spare the time.

Song of the Rockies

The Rockies sing to us at sunrise
    when crystal snow-capped peaks
chant iridescent matins to the dawn,
    the dawn of a fresh new mountain day.

Luminous pastel clouds
    hover across the horizon
painting the hills and valleys below
    in mysterial shades of
lavender, amber and rose.

The Rockies sing to us at daybreak
    when every crest and vale
unites in raising anthems to the dawn,
    The dawn of a bright new mountain morn.

Forests and fields awaken.
    A bull elk grazes by an alpine lake.
An eagle soars through the morning mist
    over rainbows of mountain paintbrush.
A hilltop lake spills over its rim
    and cascades down the slope
etching serpentine streams in the valley below.

We can hear the mountains singing.
  In every creature, ridge and flower
They bring to us their jubilant songs
  of wilderness, wildlife and wonder.

We can hear the Rockies singing.
  The mountains sing forever!

Autumn Finale

Spare no lament for the maple leaves
    that hail their impending fall
with blazing gold and scarlet concerts
    bright as Christmas brass in marble halls.

How bold their radiant hymns resound -
    mute to the sweatered ones below
whose treble scraping rakes -
    raise smoldering pyres of the fallen.

Steamy plumes from cocoa mugs
    blend with burning oak and maple wisps
as rakers chant their own sweet airs,
    "The colors surprised this year,
didn't think we'd had the rain."

So spare no lament for the maple leaves
    whose jubilant anthems,
raised beneath the harvest moon,
    herald their fall with rainbow alleluias.

Eagles on the Mississippi

Majestic eagles ride on thermals high
   above the river's wooded shore:
white hooded monarchs of the sky.

Keen eyes survey the waters as they fly
   in quest of prey to taste or store.
Majestic eagles ride on thermals high.

Above the bluffs, their shadows multiply
   as each December dawn brings more
white hooded monarchs to the sky.

At winter's end they'll homeward fly
   to fish the river's northern corridor.
Majestic eagles ride on thermals high.

The eagle's noble span and piercing cry
   are immortalized in native lore.
White hooded monarchs rule the sky!

Since on spirit wings I must rely
   I dream aloft where eagles soar
and glide with them on thermals high:
   white hooded monarchs of the sky.

Dolphin Ballet

A graceful water weaving dolphin
swirls wakes of gentle waves -
a white, silver blue phantom
shimmering in the noonday sun.

Piercing the surface,
she dances an aquatic ballet
of corkscrew pirouettes
and majestic somersaults.

Diving beneath the spray
she churns her engine upward -
soaring through the flaming hoop
to the *"oohs"* and applause
of a throng of short-sleeved hominids
bleachered beyond the rails.

Plunging into quiet depths,
she lingers for a moment
perhaps to recall the fresh sea air
and the borderless waters
in the golden days before the ships came.

Lodgepole Pines

Resting couched and cross-legged
by the hearth at Old Faithful Inn,
I read of fire-seared Montana.
My restive mind roams back
a century before
to when flames ruled Yellowstone -
cracking open Lodgepole cones -
spending seeds on blackened soil.

Youthful pines soared skyward:
tutored by seven score seasons
of showers, frost and sun
nourished by leaf-meal and char.

Then loggers came to notch their trunks
and sent them arcing to the forest floor.
Carpenters fixed them to the wall
where the moose head stares me down.

Montana pinecones crackle as I read.
After soaking rains have quenched the flames,
those seeds will rise to giant towers
then yield to the whine of loggers' saws.

A gray haired man will enter
a rustic Montana lodge,
a coffee mug clutched in one hand,
the morning paper in the other
and sit fire-warmed by a granite hearth
set in a wall of Lodgepole Pines.

13 Ways of Looking at the Mountains

homage to Wallace Stevens

I - My Focus pistoned up the rise
    and all at once, the Rockies -
        silhouettes against the western skies.

II - On the road to Boulder
    a pleated ridge crawls north
        like a blue whale bound for the open sea.

III - Appalachia's intoxicating verdure
    never fails to induce in us
        a certain mellowing of the spirit.

IV - You 'conquered' my North Face, did you?
    Why, I should skewer your arrogant ass
        like a holiday lamb culled for the sacrifice.

V - Lewis and Clark looked west
    surveying the Bitterroots' frigid expanse.
        Farewell Northwest Passage!

VI - Pueblos stranded on Enchanted Mesa -
    their rock stairs crumbled to the valley floor.
        Should they dive to their death or starve?

VII - Touristas at Big Bend Park
    wonder at its pastel window -
        its romantic haze a toxic gift
    from stacks across the Rio Grande.

VIII – The once mighty Ozarks humbled by age,
    dwarfed by the youthful Rockies.
        Listen up, youngsters, your time will come!

IX – We de-bussed to seize the dolomites
    with our hyper-kinetic shutters.
        Pausing for a draught of Italian air,
    I felt the whack of an Alpine snowball.

X - Before Oregon's crater had its lake,
    Volcanic fury scorched the village below.
        Today its azure waters preach only serenity.

XI – Looking down from Shissler peak
    to the golden meadow below
        where the elk herd calmly grazes.

XII – Do mists veil the Blue Ridge Mountains
    or are there really no mountains at all -
        only clouds decked out in mountain attire?

XIII – They say that peaks more steep than Everest
    soar up from the ocean floor.
        Who will scale their sunken heights?

The Master Weaver

In the calm still moonlit night
    she silently wove a silken tapestry -
       spinnerets spewing slender strands
   light as air but strong as Kevlar.

A silvery armature spanned the trail
  clinging to trunks and branches.
      Rappelling down from its pinnacle,
  she fixed radii to her deadly wheel.

Spiraling in from the outer ring
    she knitted her way to the center
      to await the tell-tale shudder
 of a fly or moth flown into her snare.

She took no note of the hiker
   paused alone on the trail -
     transfixed by the dew laden spiral
 shimmering in the rose-glow sun.

It mattered not to the spider
   that a man would find her work pleasing
     and it mattered not to the man
 that the web was not woven for art.

Cloudburst

Barreling through town
in the depth of night,
earth's colossal magnets
hurled jagged fire spears -
flashing and ripping the midnight sky.

Whirling torrents whistled
and lashed against the glass.
A blinding fire bolt
Shattered an old rock maple -
quaking our shelter to its footings.

Cosmic strobe-lit concussions
stuttered and roared across the nightscape
like a feral timpanist gone mad.

The frenzied cacophony
subsided at last -
rumbled off in the distance
as the storm lumbered on
like a barbarian horde
off to sack another village.

Tranquility
at the Missouri Botanical Garden

The earth paused in its orbit
that peaceful autumn afternoon
as we strolled the garden paths
cloaked beneath a veil of cotton clouds.

We walked through a kaleidoscope
of hanging globes of spectral mums,
Hypericum patches lined the trail -
their red berries exploding into golden stars
and sartorial toad lilies had
donned their finest freckles.

Across the garden lake,
grasses, maples and burning bush
embellished the opposite shore.
a maple leaf floated by
like a delicate raft
painted gold with scarlet trim.

This was the hour the world stood still
in the tranquil grace
of an autumn afternoon.

Growing Season

for Greg Guenther

A giant pendulum in the cosmos swings
    as galactic pinwheels whirl in the aether.
Earth's axis inclines towards fairer weather
    and gentle rains presage new beginnings.

Crocuses push the snow aside, a skylark sings
    of light and darkness held in equal measure.
Pastel fingers on every bough appear
    while birds and beasts pursue their matings.

Rain softened fields greet the tillers' blades
    submerging seeds for the rain and sun
to raise into fields of corn and wheat.

The pendulum arcs back and summer fades
    as Earth's axis slants to a cooler inflection
and farmers bow thanks for the harvest complete!

Beethoven's Walk

(Scene by the brook)

He came seeking solace to Heiligenstadt
   and walked alone by its crystal stream
      welcomed by songs the nightingale taught.

Its cheerful waters made Vienna seem
   a distant, cool and forbidding stage
      where few would embrace a pastoral dream.

He dotted his sketchbooks on every page
   with earthen tones born of peasant heart -
      (though fare rich enough for any age) .

He poured from the stream the fiddle part,
   and woodwinds sang with the birds in the dell -
      all "choired" together by the master's art.

At Heiligenstadt Beethoven attended well
   and bequeathed us his golden 'Pastorale.'

Chrysalis

I doubt the humble caterpillar
has any premonition
of the glory that awaits her
on her impending coronation day.

Newly hatched, she meanders
over leaves and stalks, binging on the crawl,
in quest of the perfect hanging leaf.

Then suddenly metamorphosis
and silk is everywhere
wrapping her up like Nefertiti -
her insides churned into enzyme soup
a new essence in the making.

Shaking, writhing, a bold new self
Is emerging deep within
an orange and black-winged butterfly
waiting for that liberating hour
to shed her crumbling shell
and beat the air with new- found wings.

Grand Canyon

Two billion years ago
the river we call Colorado
opened a gash in the Kaibab crust

sculpting sandstone, granite, and limestone spectra
on the rugged canyon walls -
reflecting the searing Arizona sun.

Millennial torrents scoured the plain.
Juniper and Aspen, torn from the expanding banks,
sucked into the river's red-stained vortex.

All the while the restless Colorado,
obedient to gravity's law,
scoured its bed a mile below the rim.
The last dinosaur perished - choked by volcanic soot.

Pangaea rumbled, groaned and split
and an eye-blink ago our African parents
stood to take their first faltering steps.

Their progeny crossed the Bering bridge
roaming south to build stone shelters
tucked against these canyon walls.

Did the Havasupai huddle in fright
of the jagged firelight searing the skies –
pounding the air across the hollows?

And emerging at storm's end
did they gaze at the rainbow mist
spread over the buttes and valleys?

After dusk, with fires withering to embers,
did they rest supine,
heads pillowed on their arms,
pondering the jewel case universe?

Alpenglow

Dusk descends across the west
    as our yellow dwarf star
surrenders its daily reign -
    washing the horizon
in a diadem of refracted light.

Prismatic clouds blaze
    like a wondrous skycape
brushed by an impressionist deity-
    conjoining the passing day
with the emerging veil of night.

The first stars have arrived
    to escort the silvery moon
along its nocturnal journey.

The season of sleep is upon us.
    A few tilts of the hour glass
will transport our circling furnace
    just below the eastern peaks -
a harbinger of the coming day.
    Dawn and twilight
framed in luminous Alpenglow.

Part II – MUSIC OF THE SPHERES

Boundaries of Time and Space

The sun boils off its heat-light flares
      93,000,000 miles away
            yet as close to us as sunburn -
      drafting the circles of our years.

Our ancestors fill our boots
      with us and our descendants
            (one pair - so many feet)
      stepping out to where we've been.

Along the corridors of time,
      our mind screens play what passed
            before we fledged and fled our nests:
      There is here and then is now.

Whether we tilt the earth to shake out
      wisdom, fame or empathy
            or let chaos light our paths,
      our curiosity is a sturdy ladder raised

to scale the walls of space and time.
      Who cares that life presages death and
            decay calls breath from dust?
      Our earthly sojourns - our souls' domain.

Out of Chaos

Shall we pause to consider
the shudder of a butterfly's wings
that sets the hurricane spinning
or the descent of the final raindrop
that breaches the groaning levy?

Shall we ponder the moment before
a chorus of "maybe's" morphs
into the vain eloquence of history?

Roiling in the broth of chaos
a cluster of causes startles the surface -
unfurling queues of effects
that dot the time-scape
like rows of teetering dominoes.

Typhoons twist villages to ruins,
armies rise to victory or
fall to the earth in despair,
or a medical miracle is born
from the agile mind of a doctor
conceived in a Chevy's back seat.

So here we stand on the ridge of time
ourselves both caused and causing,
cradling the sphere of chaos in our hands -
uncertain what effect will be our being
after all our causes are enumerated.

Time will surely tell - as soon
as we tell time exactly what to say.

Cenozoic Me

Our mystic alabaster satellite
rules the midnight sky
casting shadowy silhouettes
of all our trees and houses.

Rational *tri-millennial* me
chooses not to bay about it
or worship its fabled godly essence
(long since neutered by geology).

Casting aside the chains of time
I sidle up to *Cenozoic* me
munching on a leg of venison
staring at that improbable hanging ball
suspended in the southern heavens.

Wonder and vexation cloud his hairy face -
hunting vainly for a clue.
I whisper in a secret tongue
that only he and I can comprehend,
"You may not get it yet, grandpa
but soon enough you will."

Looking Glass Universe

A looking glass seems such a simple thing -
a boomerang of sorts
tossing back the you that others see.

So many me's (or you's) to view -
bucked out in natal garb
or gussied up for the corporate ball.
Better fix my Medusa hair,
Should I opt for the purple shirt?
Just who will I seem to be to you today?

Take a breath - a really deep one:
meet those soul panes
gazing back from the other side
emissaries from an inverted universe -
romancing the past -
stalked by tomorrow's "maybes".

Who will I chance to serve or sway or fool
between now and the evening star?
Will one of them be you or me?

A looking glass seems such a simple thing.
So many me's (or you's) to view,
Just who should I seem to be to me today?

Eternal Dust

Cradling a handful of Illinois dust,
dry residue of sycamore, deer
and ancient Mississippians,
I splay my fingers like an eagle's claw -
releasing it to the fickle breezes.

A sudden gust of wind
swirls up an ocher cloud -
a cyclone dervish of sand and clay.

My hand, upraised for a shield
ever so briefly vanishes -
veiled by the impatient dust.

Centrifugal Force

Before our circles close and seal
Their arcs,

What leaks out into the frigid void?

What is sucked in like a
careless insect

Caught!
In a fly trap's eager mouth?

What clusters near the
center

warmed by its radiant nucleus?

Who or what bangs on the
perimeter

Shouting for entry or exodus?

Who is the guardian of
the gate?

What theorems
govern the geometry
of the psyche?

The Fly on Einstein's Wall

If I could be a fly on Einstein's wall
I'd buzz about from chair to curtain
watch him check out plans and gadgets
and scratch remarks on his papers.
When the clock edged noon
his stomach would growl,
he'd fold up the prints and say,
"It's a relatively short walk to the café."

With Albert out I'd take the run of the place -
practicing banks and dips and vertical lifts.
I'd munch on scraps of Brie and fowl
left fused to the edge of his table.

When the tumblers turned
I'd buzz back to my wall, eager to witness
whatever this sage would chance to say.
He'd go to his desk to file reports
and stack them neatly into a tray.

Without warning he'd rise from his chair
scattering papers across the floor.

"MASS AND ENERGY ARE ONE, " he'd shout, -
"CRUSHED TOGETHER BY TIME! "

I'd buzz and swoop and fly circles and loops
and taxi in on his collar.
I'd beat my wings to cool his brain.

But wait…Whose voice do I hear?
Oh, it's you gentle reader.
"Stop, hold it right there, damned pest!
It couldn't have happened that way!
Have you no shame or respect for God's truth? "

But I'd stare you down with my compound eye
and scornfully twitch my wings.
Consider this, troubled sir,
you're the one scolding a talking fly.

Emergence

Before first life –
a sea of primal broth.

Before the child –
a seeded egg shook and split.

Before men spoke –
only utterance and signs.

Before bridled fire –
a raw and frigid world.

Before awareness
subsistence sufficed.

With reflection
came experience recalled.

Myriad thresholds
reached and transcended.

From every this, something else
otherwise and unexpected.

How strange that we
move our pens to essence.

Stranger still
that we are here at all.

Space Shuttle

Jimmy Collins made a dash for the door
Shouting to the silhouettes at the bar,
"Lock up for me boys, the baby's coming."
All the men cheered
And struck their glasses together.

Relief and joy swept over Rose and Jimmy
The memory of that arduous passage
Fading under the light of resplendent love
Asleep in her mother's arms.

*   *   *   *   *   *   *   *   *   *

The radio crackled and spoke,
"Houston to 'Endeavor, '
Good morning, Commander Collins."
And Eileen fell out of one dream into another.
Beyond her window a hazy blue ball spun slowly.

How was it possible for the Earth to be "there"
And for "here" to be any place else?

200 miles below James and Rose
Looked up in wonder at the sky.

A Retroactive Question

Stephen Hawking in a fantasy rush
once thought the universe would max its tether,
turn a mighty one eighty back toward
the starting gun and run the show in reverse.

What if it were really so?

Would a butterfly return to pre-chrysalis days,
crawl backwards on stalks and un-munch leaves?

Would Frost back-step that diverged path
to ponder his options anew?

Would we jettison those data circuits
that school has stuffed inside us
and retreat to our amniotic broth?

What if it were really so?

Uh oh, here come the terrible lizards
back for a curtain call.
Don't you think it's getting awfully hot?

What if it were really so?

Imagine if you can, the silence following the
great "thwupping" sound of the "gnaB giB".

Old Boethius

Anicius Manlius Severinus Boethius wrote his tripartite definition of music in a prison cell awaiting execution in AD 524.

Musica Instrumentalis

Supple tunes with dulcet harmonies,
echoing through the hills and forests
soothe, enliven and assure us all
with nascent thoughts of unity.
Deep within its tonal weave
a soft voice whispers, *"there is more."*

Music Humana

Bound within our pliant shells
with pumps and bones and sinews joined
chants an elemental litany, *"You are one"!*
Spun from helices of DNA.
our throats and tongues are set to motion
raising pleas to heaven, *"Tell us more!"*

Musica Mundana

Harmony reigns in interstellar space
with all in motion – all in place.
Celestial choirs with essence energy,
tuned and voiced to gravity's cosmic chords,
sing with interstellar euphony,
"We are music of the spheres from which all others spring."

PART III – GLOBAL FAMILY PICNIC

Human Family Picnic

dedicated with hope to all of us

Imagine a Human Family Picnic
where everyone shows -
from every sect and hue and nation -
gathered at a common table.

The Almighty swoops down
to speak the blessing:
known to all from Torah, Q'uran and Gospels
and countless other books of wisdom -
author of our souls' aspirations.

After supper the Holy One
would call us to the sacrificial pyre.

>   *"Brothers, sisters and cousins,*
>   *Images of your creator,*
>   *every unholy war*
>   *desecrates the face of God*
>   *and there is no other kind.*
>   *Cast your pride into the flames*
>   *and live together in peace!"*

Obediently, we'd toss our
pride in the fire,
recoiling from its smoldering stench.
The Lion would lie down to preen the Lamb's fleece
and *Universal Love*, released from her chains,
would walk free in every land.

Affirmation

for Nat Lipstadt

She smiled as she
set her lips into
most agreeable motion -
her larynx flexing to
modulate the passing air.

The sequenced air waves
shook his auric drums
and journeyed to his soul.

Out of his reservoir
of ritual response
his lower face
turned a congenial curve.

Two puffs of air
pulsed his vocal folds,
were filtered
by tongue, teeth and lips
and formed a sonic pattern
she was sure to know,

"Thank you."

Horizontal Transcendence

for Dr. Ursula Goodenough

To better view the fairest stars of
Genesis, Keats or Kepler,
the priests of vertical transcendence
built towers over clouds -
beyond the touch of worldly toil.

Standing below in soiled boots,
newer prophets citing
the universal brotherhood of
mitosis, chromosomes and DNA,
urge a new transcendence
spread on a horizontal plain
where bridges are preferred to ladders.

Muffled distant drums,
beating somber warnings
of poisoned waters and global heat,
summon us down
from our lofty towers of denial.

Murmuring rhythms of forests and streams
and all species of flora and fauna
line out the same life beats
as the engines in our chests.
The God without is the God within -
nestled within our nuclei.

With global death within the grasp
of our reckless finger tips,
and bullet fever
infesting our earthly villages,
are we ready yet
to yield a measure of our trust
to the healing power
of horizontal transcendence?

Mightiest of Swords

I - WORDS LIKE PRISMS

The crystal awaits the perfect slant of sun.
The world turns just so and refracted light
Hurls a color blaze against the wall.

So it is when a long awaited word
Forms on the lips of the wise.

II - WORDS LIKE FLAX

In the flames of conflict
Words fall to the floor like mounds of charred flax
Red-faced saints gather clumps to themselves
To spin into finest thread for self-flattering raiment.

III - WORDS WITHOUT WORDS

When pain burrows deep in the marrow
Where words cannot assuage
A gentle touch can bleed some out
And channel hope back in.
No words can spell a kind caress.

IV - POISON WORDS

Beware the charismatic
Carrying a jar of poison pills
Cover your glass when he passes your way
Or he'll slip one in unawares.

V - LAUGHING WORDS

Absurdities and failures are the stuff of jokes.
Long live *non sequiturs* and *double entendres!*
We love a clumsy tumble into the drink
As long as no one drowns.

VI - WORDS FOR BUILDING

Of course you can!
I place my total trust in you.

VII - WORD PAINTING

Mister Frost's words never made a wood
Or caused a harness bell to shake.
Even so I'd travel many miles
To see his imagined snow accumulate.

VIII - THE GIFT

My cat, Zoe, never says a word to me!
He doesn't have the tongue or lips or larynx for it.
He cannot fit his paws around a pen.
His brain's too small for metaphors.

The gift belongs to us alone.
To craft words to build or kill or heal.

Forgive us Zoe for doing little with so much.

Alone

How could I ever understand
what it is you choose
to call existence
and how could I ever
tell you what it means to me?

A solitary dot stained
on the canvas
of the expanding universe,
I sense a primal shiver
whenever, 'stranger'
cries out from a page
or whispers in the aether.

Life be not Proud

When proud ones boast
Of all that is loftiest
In his faith,
In her flag,
In the hue of their skin
The Devil licks his chops
In lustful salivation.

When caring souls
Reach out to offer
A bowl of rice,
A healing dose,
An understanding ear,
An open heart
Satan clutches his dry throat
Gasping for air.

Miracles without Marquees

Take me to a miracle
I asked of "no one in particular."

Give me a philharmonic in the sky
and a blazing talking bush.

Let me see a virgin's ghost
and a lame man dance a jig.

I'd like to catch the show just once
before I flee this vale of fears!

Then no one in particular chided me
called me "vanity's clown."

Still, I tried to call him out
in the realm where words are born.

I thought that if I could crack the code of
how a vision breaks the void.

or how a proud and callous tongue
can raise a sanguine humor

or how a toddler breaks the silence
with his first astounding word,

then I'd topple "no one in particular"
from his lofty station!

But alas I failed to own the source
of a solitary thought or word

or what it means to care or conjure
or why I came to seek a miracle.

A hidden voice from nowhere in particular
gently slaked my feeble pride,

"Surrender to each dawn and dusk;
they're all the miracles you need."

Transcendental Etude

Our footsteps echo through ancient halls,
  where here is everywhere
and every time is now.

Caesar's twin-edged conquests are our own
  as is Brutus's fickle knife
and Marc Anthony's cunning speech.

Plague steals across our Europe
  like a remorseless highwayman -
rosies all ringed and falling down.

We wait in Wien's Kärntnertor theater
  for Schiller's *An die Freude*
to shine anew in Beethoven's score

and are ushered in at Menlo Park
  where Edison's tungsten faintly glows.
Tomorrow will bring sun to the night.

There's Jonas Salk at his microscope.
  One more test will crack the code
to banish polio's savage scourge.

But nature's caprice strews logs on our roads.
  We are dashed by a Tsunami's rage.
Katrina's torrents have swallowed our homes.

Prides of warriors wade rivers of blood
    and Darfur bullets tear into our chests.
Nuclear Toys 'R Us shelves are fully stocked.

We are the heirs of every triumph and treachery.
    We grasp the keys to tomorrow.
    What have we done? What must we do?

Step right up!

I stand on tip toes in the circle
- grasping for the ring.

It slips - drops - clangs.
(Oh dear you saw that, didn't you -
witness to my futility)?

Go ahead then take a turn.
Curve your knuckles
reach out - seize the brass!

Did you miss again?

What the hell,
let's go another round
for bending or for broke.

The clock ticks on -
soon enough
we'll both be was.
Today is for the seizing.

Unity Tree

```
T                               R
  I                         E
    M                   T
      E               T
        *           A
          M
        BECOMING
          Y
        G       S
      R           P
    E               A
  N                   C
E                       E
```

Fugitive Visions

Life is a Cafeteria

Life is like a cafeteria because
you have to stand in line
when you're hungry.

Anatomy of Arrogance

A shivering ball of fear,
wrapped in a crust of pride
too thick for sharpest arrows,
huddles alone but well protected

hoping beyond all dread
that none will ever come to know
the terror behind the mask.

Modern Narcissis

Narcissus leaned forward
to better view his matchless beauty
and tumbled to watery doom.

Beloved America,
how far can we lean in self adoration
before our coasts tilt into the seas?

Combo

Come join our combo,
but just so you know,
we all *comp* for each other,
take a chorus now and then
and try to keep up with the changes.

Like a Phoenix

Courageous Phoenix, what do you know
of past and future conflagrations?
With wings afire, do you sense
the embers of your renascent soul?
Is your savage life-death vortex
as mysterious to you as it is to us?

Although I'll never fly on Phoenix wings,
or share your tortured falls and resurrections,
I feel I know you as a brother
for we all have Phoenix games to play
with each dividing and perishing cell
its own ancestor and descendant -
tomorrow's joys born of present sorrows.

Who among us has never tasted
the bitter gall of enmity -
or been driven to our knees
by the searing blade of failure?

Noble Phoenix, in our barren seasons
when scorched spirits tumble to the earth,
soar down from your blackened rock
and restore the feathers of our tattered wings.

Canticle of Hope

The whole earth resounds
with the exuberant songs
of nature's majestic harmony.

And sways to the steady pulse
of all that breathes and roams the land,
that inhabits the rushing brooks
or soars through borderless skies,
of every seedling, flower and chrysalis.
And every newborn calf and golden field.
all that rise to greet the sun
intone their festal hymns
to nature's exultant harmony.

The boundless wonders of nature's realm,
sustain our spirits and illumine our paths
with wisdom taught by the lakes and mountains
and solace sung by the forests and plains.
So with steady and transfigured hearts,
we forge our trails through hallowed land.

When the sun has run its daily course
and when twilight claims the fading light,
we offer thanks for the nascent moon
and the radiant star-jeweled night -
tuning our faith and aspirations
to the music of the spheres.

The whole earth resounds
with the exuberant songs
of nature's majestic harmony.

PART IV: ANCIENT FOOTPRINTS

Lame Deer's Vision

High atop the mountain
a boy crouched alone in the vision pit – waiting.
Raising his red stone pipe to the four directions
he sent clouds of willow bark smoke
skyward toward his ancestors.

Naked beneath his star blanket he wept a man's cry –
crying for a vision to come
that his people might live!
Chanting with eyes fast shut he waited and prayed.

First came the cries of the wind,
then the whisper of trees.
Birds swooped and circled about him.
He shook his rattle crying,
"Tunkashila, grandfather spirit, help me."

A voice spoke in the call of a bird,
*"Your sacrifice will make you, Wikasa Wakan, medicine man.
We are the winged ones and we are your brothers."*

In a swirling cloud his great, grandfather came and spoke,
blood dripping from the hole
where a white soldier's bullet had found his chest,
"You will take my name, Tahka Ushte, Lame Deer."
The new man on the mountain rejoiced.

Quietly entering the vision pit,
kind Old Chest placed a hand on Lame Deer's shoulder,
"Four days have passed, it is time."
and led Tahka Ushte down to the valley.

Sipapu

At the third world's first sun,
the Anasazi climbed
through a narrow Sipapu
and pressed footprints in the dust
of a new unspoiled universe.

In secluded canyon hollows
watered by softly chanting springs,
they piled rocks upon stones
shaping vast adobe cities
mortared with pastes of moistened clay.

At Mesa Verde - Chaco - de Chelly
fields of maize sway,
brushed by the canyon winds
while Pueblos danced in the plazas below
to the throbbing beats
of skin-stretched hollow log drums.

Today their children's children
circle fire pits in sacred Kivas
raising chants and prayers
to their hallowed ancestors.

Wearied by famine and conquest,
Pueblo eyes scan the heavens
searching for a new Sipapu
to lead them to a better world still.

Mastodon Hunt

Spear shafts splintering beneath its hulk -
the mastodon crashed to the earth,
roared its final lament and fell silent.

Shouts echoed across the ravine.
Dark-haired Clovis hunters converged:
stripping the hide,
carving the flesh.

Others frenzied about the carcass,
tracing broken shafts
to salvage flint for tomorrow's hunt -
retrieving all save one.

A triumphal fire hissed and snapped,
hurling heat and smoke
high into the mid-day sky.

*   *   *   *   *   *   *   *   *   *   *   *   *

*The archaeologist dropped to his knees
To brush away the millennial dust
and raised the flint find to the sun
shouting, "Clovis point"!*

Khaki and blue -jeaned hunters gathered quickly
to read the epic in flint and bone:
Mastodon and Clovis
united by the point of a spear.
"Clovis point" – an epiphany in the dust!

Cahokia Solstice

At Woodhenge's sacred circle
Hut-roused Mississipians
gathered in wintery bleakness
to track the golden crown's
ascent above the solstice post.

Their Solar Priest presided:
explaining,
blessing,
interpreting,
and assuring them all
that tomorrow's sun would rise
slightly farther to the north.

Last solstice morn at Cahokia,
latter day Mississippians
observed our red dwarf star
as it broke the tree - clad horizon,
inclined slightly to the right
and soared into cold December's sky.

Our Sun Priest, robed
in a ranger's jacket
in his own way:
explained,
blessed,
interpreted
and released us
to our journeys home -

assured that tomorrow's sun
again would climb the heavens
slightly farther to the north.

Missouri Triptych

Western Sources

Mist, rain and snowmelt gather
And soak the Montana crests.
A trio of rivulets carves the slopes,
Grow to rivers that braid into a single course
And the Missouri is born at Three Forks.

Shoshone and Hidatsu rest from the hunt,
Kneel and cup their hands
To raise life giving liquid to their lips
While horses bow beside them
Bellies filled with the refreshing waters.

The river flows north dividing the tall grasslands,
Plunges over the cataracts at Great Falls,
Churns on the rocks below
And drives inexorably toward the sea.

Mandan and Sioux

Soft flute sounds drift from the Mandan village
Intertwining with the riffling music of the river.
By its banks a coarse French trapper roasts a rabbit
To share with his Shoshone child-bride.
Sacagawea sings softly beside him -
Charboneau's son stirring in her womb.

Sioux warriors on horseback
Stand guard by the shores.
How many travelers have passed?
How many are yet to come?
Beyond the rolling hills
A buffalo stumbles and falls
Pierced by Lakota arrows and spears.

Boats in the Water

At *River du Bois* where the Missouri
Collides with the Mississippi,
Forty men slip into boats and take to the oars
To interpret Jefferson's continental dream -
Their keelboat laden with sustenance,
Herbs, weapons and powder.
They carry trinkets to dazzle the natives
And cast bronze medals to give them
Bearing images of their "Father in Washington"
That none had asked to have.

Terror in her Eyes

Sacagawea's Capture

As I strolled the Knife River trail
a dust cloud swirled and fell
and earth lodges appeared by the score
extending from the path to the river banks.

Hidatsa women sang at their chores,
    husking corn -
        beading moccasins -
            scraping a buffalo hide.

A band of hunters dismounted
and released their ropes -
dropping two deer and an elk
by the hanging rack.

Triumphal shouts from the river
turned all heads to the shore
where warriors, fresh back
from Shoshone fields,
lashed up canoes and dragged
their human spoils up the rise.

Several squaws reached out
from the gathering crowd
seizing two of the squirming children.

A Shoshone girl with terror in her eyes
cringed as a warrior raised his arm.

"No, tell your Hidatsa name!"
Sobbing she choked through broken tears,
"My name is Sacagawea."

I bolted to breach the walls of time
to face death in her defense
but a new whirling cloud intervened.

When the dust fell away
all the lodges had vanished
with all the Hidatsa villagers.

Kneeling down to the Dakota grass,
I caressed a circular hollow
etched deeply in the silent earth.

Carved Granite

The Brick Church Road leads to Friedens
where yesterday as today
wooden carts and steel wagons,
ferry their most solemn cargo.

After the preacher's comfort tonings
of walks through the shadowy valley
and eyes lifted to the hills,
After fresh sod flourishes
over the sealed earth,
the carved stones whisper,

"Remember our bearings and sirings,
the banners we carried,
our triumphs and stumblings.
Sound the words and tunes of our jubilant songs!
Never forget that we are you."

Vesuvius: Bonito and the Tour Guide

(Plaster cast at Pompeii)

[THE TOUR GUIDE]

> *"Ladies and gentlemen, here we are at*
> *Pompeii's fabled Thermal Baths where*
> *heated water was passed through duct work*
> *in the walls. One can imagine Nero himself*
> *stopping here on one of his visits."*

[BONITO]

Bonito stepped out of the bathhouse and looked up.
Vesuvius rumbled - shaking ash and fire skyward.
Breaking into a run he sought the south road,
glancing back anxiously at the
vast dark cloud billowing down the mountain.

> *"The principal city roads were recessed and wagons were*
> *fitted with standardized wheelbases and clearances to*
> *fit in channels cut into the stone. Follow me, please to the*
> *residential area."*

He gained the road and his feet
pounded the stones of the "via stabiana."
The cloud multiplied and fell on the city.
Ever deepening layers of ash clogged Benito's path.
Heart pounding in his chest he lengthened his strides

"Leaving the opulent villas with their spacious atria, we
now enter the market area where we shall see a display of
remarkable interest.
During excavations, empty spaces were discovered in the ash
deposits."

The rising ash captured his left leg.
Bonito inhaled the fiery air and thrust
forward into a burst of falling soot
but was unable to finish his stride.

"Archaeologists poured plaster into the voids revealing the
outlined bodies of Pompeiins trapped in their final
moments. Take, for example, this man caught in mid-step with
no time to escape the life - choking dust."

Harper's Ferry

A bell tolled
through the fog at dusk
to summon passage
across the roiling waters.

Through the mist
a ferry appeared
but not the same as called -
afoul with death and sorrow.

With dread our forefathers
boarded ship and listened through
that storm filled crossing
to howling wind-sung requiems
echoing from distant fields at
Manassus - Shiloh - Gettysburg.

When the gales had spent their fury
they disembarked in a new land
with both far less and more
than they left on the opposite shore.

V - A PLACE TO CALL HOME

A Time for Flying

Flight came so easily
when I was a boy of seven.

I'd hover over sidewalks, cars and lawns
gliding on a sea of azure air
above my friends at play
and Mom and Pop talking on the stoop.

I'd circle over McKinley School (my school)
where the recess bell is ringing
and the creek by the edge of the woods
where I found the railroad flare
(my creek, my woods).

Flight came ever so easily
when I was seven (or was it eight?)
when the sky was autumn blue
and the world below was kind and true.

But in time, science grounded me,
said it was just a dream.
After all a boy can't just up
and repeal the law of gravity, can he?

Why yes, of course he can:
it comes so easy
when you're seven or eight
and the skies are right for flying.

Songbird

For Robin

Robin hums as she tends her garden
while birds perch all around
waiting for rustling seeds
to fill the slender columns.
Humming birds hover
to sip sweet nectar mixed for them alone.

On concert nights her voice takes flight.
and fills the hall with her radiant soul.
On quiet mornings
graphite joins with paper
and a flower's form and meaning
are captured by her vision.

A friend fallen ill or reeling from loss
receives her gift of comfort words
and a card or meal soon follows.

Grandchildren rush to greet her
and happily fill her arms.
at night they cloak themselves
In love quilts sewn by Grandma's hands.

If you want to learn how love abides
or long to know its fullness
follow my Robin for a day
Her gift is in the gifting.

Living Brahms

in loving memory of my mother

Three simple cello notes answered by horns,
rising and falling winds
shine like the dawn of a luminous day.
Emergent violins wash the hall
with mystic Austrian radiance.

Looking across the stage
I meet the eyes of my Philharmonic friends
uniting in affirmation
of the haunting largesse
of the Brahms' second -
our collective soul vaulting the Atlantic
to the azure Danube's shore.

> *It's 40 Christmas morns ago*
> *and I am "20-ish" tearing floral paper*
> *from a large green book and lean*
> *to give my Mom a thank you hug.*

Three quarters of an hour
brush by like an autumn breeze
and I close that same green book
and turn to greet the audience -
searching beyond the walls
for that sacred somewhere
where Mom smiles down
from her eternal resting place.

Slicing a Banana

I sliced a fresh banana today
    alone at my kitchen counter.

I drew a common table knife
    and carved a slender yellow disc
that lingered on the blade.

The next disc drove it off the knife
    and down to the cereal below.

Soon the banana was all partitioned
    and the Cheerios mostly masked.
I popped the heel in my mouth.

Childhood memories crackle
    like a radio slightly off its station
      and I can almost hear mom
    talking softly as she slices -

I am barely listening.
    My left hand holds an imaginary banana
      while my right hand maneuvers
    a non-existent knife.

How strange the knife I held so real
    yet the shade of mom merely conjured -
far too strange to truly believe.

Thelma's World

Early spring has come to Thelma's farm.
The geese are on the pond,
a green velvet carpet circles the barn
while songbirds greet the morning sun.

We walk down Thelma's rutted road
where milk trucks used to rumble in
to fetch the morning's yield.
Old Tikki leads the way - a pale fluff of a mutt
like a dust mop searching for its handle.

Thelma's cows are long since gone –
sold off after Dutch was called to eternity
but she'd no more forsake this land - her land
than the sun would forget to rise.

Early spring has come to the Missouri hills
where clean warm breezes whisper hope.
Soon the ready soil will taste
the furrowing blades of the plow
near fields where livestock graze and flourish.

We've reached the bend in the road.
Old Tikki's wearing down
so we turn to retrace our steps.
A committee of neighbor calves
studies us with soulful eyes
and we appear to pass inspection.

Tikki guides us on our homeward path
where a ribbon of golden jonquility
neatly trims the foreyard fence.

Spring has come again to Thelma's farm
as it always has and always will -
where clean warm breezes whisper hope.

Night at the Philharmonic - 1877

Snowfall gently covered Belleville
in a blanket of softest down —
iridescent in the gaslight coronas.

A carriage pulled up at City Park Hall where
the coachman took white-gloved hands
and eased the ladies gently down the steps.
Some paused to pat the horses
in thanksgiving for the lift.

Top - hatted men offered arms to their wives,
escorting them up the snowy stairs
and into the buzzing lobby.

Trays of wine circled the room -
their cargo reduced at every stop.
Each raconteur spoke of celebration for the
Philharmonic had turned a decade old that week.

Programs in hand, people claimed their seats
while musicians on stage
practiced random admixtures of
excerpts that would come to order soon.

Then by the light of gas chandeliers,
Julius Liese raised his arms and brought
Haydn's symphonic London to Illinois -
a citizen orchestra led by the local lumber czar.

After the final echoes melted into applause
and coats were lifted over shoulders;
the time had come for the waiting carriages -
snow still swirling in the gaslight glow.

The clopping of hooves on cobblestone
drifted into the passengers' ears
and co-mingled with the echoes of
strings, drums and wind blown music
still singing in their memories
and irradiating their souls.

Pictures at an Exhibition

Poor Viktor Hartmann!
All that remained of his towering soul
were visions pressed on to paper
hanging in a St. Petersburg gallery.

Mussorgsky advanced his lumbering frame
along the gallery halls
searching for his lost friend.

Sonic images formed in the composer's mind
singing replicas of Hartmann's icons:

An old castle,
Children quarreling,
An ox resisting the yoke,
The Great Gate of Kiev.

Mussorgsky's notes flourish and vanish
as ephemeral as life itself -
passing into the ether only to live anew
with each successive performance.

Viktor lives!

En Passant

The 64 squares on a chessboard
match the tally of my years –
some passed in red,
others in black -
another day, another game.

Mostly I prefer to play
the knight with angled junkets
cutting a dashing profile
like the head of his noble steed
(though many moves, alas,
resemble another part of the horse) .

Of course it is rather grand
to be monarch for a day
calling the shots
from a gilded throne
in a rustic medieval castle

but a mere half turn of the wheel
busts me down to humble pawn -
moving one square at a time -
rendering to Caesar his due.

Chess may not be my game of choice
but there isn't any other
and on the whole it's not so bad
save for that infernal timer!

Medicine Wagon

I'd jump at the chance to ride shotgun
on Henry's medicine wagon
rolling from city to village
hawking *'Stickin' Salve'* and *'Oil of Gladness'*.

We'd ride into Elmira's County Fair
and set up over by the lake.
I'd fix old Diamond a pail of oats
and draw her a bucket of water.
while great, great grandpa
squeezed on his Union coat
and arranged his potions on the shelves.

Henry's voice would boom
across the water like a megaphone
and people would gather close -
lured in by the old codger's
hypnotic banter of miracle cures -
and perilous Civil War battles.

He'd swear on his mother's lumbago
that *'Stickin' Salve'* works just as fine
as the lead and powder
he'd fired at Cedar Mountain.

The folks would shake with mirth
whenever he bellowed,
"I'm Henry Howard from Bunker Hill -
Never worked and never will."

Women would tug their husband's sleeves
and they'd bring me pennies and dimes.

After dusk we'd tally the coins
and latch down the wagon for the night
then sleep side by side on the grass
beneath the New England stars.

At sunrise I'd wipe his brow -
to ease him gently back
from the thunder of enemy shells
still firing in his restless sleep.

We'd cook up some bacon and biscuits,
hitch Diamond up to the wagon
then head south through the rolling hills
along the Tioga valley.
We'd breathe in the fresh country air
and tip our caps to the farmers.

If Henry would come to tap my shoulder
some promising morning in spring
and whisper "the wagon's hitched outside,"
I'd go in a Tioga minute.

Covered Bridges

A bridge is a curious thing to cover.
mile after mile of naked road –
then a wooden box over stream or ravine.

Why not cover the road instead
leaving the bridge unclothed?
But where's the romance in that, you say?

So perhaps it was fashioned for Currier and Ives
or to embellish the music
of iron shod hooves on oaken planks.

Or maybe was built as a kiosk
for fading feed and carnival posters
and jackknife glyphs of amorous initials.

No, all our covered bridges, imagined or real,
guide our passage over deadly waters –
holding us fast on the road
and safe from drowning.

Gathering Wood for the Hearth

It wasn't really John's saw
that carved the branch into logs -
its blade severing rings of time.
The saw was mine but just like his.

Resting for a spell, I thought of John:
clearing his spread by the Williamson Road,
building fences, raising his barn,
or, like me, cutting wood for the hearth.

But perhaps I didn't "think" of John at all
since he lives in each cell that I am.
He may have just stirred a little within
to recall pioneer paths we once had walked.

The long branch shortened
as John and I pistoned our arms
in unison across the centuries
slicing through time and space -
stacking fuel to warm a cold winter's night.

Virginia Reel

at the fete du bons vieux temps - Cahokia, Illinois

White clouds of rosin dust
Flew off Geoff's fiddle strings
As his earth dance
Soared above the pulsing
Of friends on bass and guitar.

Tuniced men bowed
To their bonneted ladies
Bedecked in colonial frocks.
In turn each pair sashayed
Down and up the line,
Whirled and laced their way
Through outstretched hands
Of family, friends and neighbors
Shaping an arch at line's end
For all the rest to pass beneath.

All across our country's timescape
Countless bridal pairs
Have sealed their sacraments
Spinning in the whirlwind
Of the Virginia Reel -
With each interclasping of arms
A blessing upon their unions.

Geoff lifted his bow from the strings,
And bowed with his band to receive
The applause rippling the air
Like the patter of ancestral rain
Nourishing the sweet soil
Of our common earthly essence.

Grace the Magician

for Grace and Dawn

There were no rabbit hat extractions,
floating pastel scarves,
or fluttering dove wings
but it was magic nonetheless.

Circled in the warmth
of comfort arms,
little Grace released her mouth
from her mother's breast
and broke her verbal silence,
"all done."

Of the 23,000 or more words
she will come to know,
all must supersede,
"All done."

But how much more magic
is yet to come?
Torrents of words
will tumble out bringing treasuries
of stored experience to her lips –
Questions and declarations
to shape and guide her universe.

Magic miracles
born of Grace and Providence
I hear your words dear child,
but beg to differ.
You have just begun.

The Finest Dance

for Betty and Clarrie

Betty was in paradise -
a soft smile on her angel face
eyes closed - gently swaying
with every note and word,

   "It's very clear, our love is here to stay,"

Why had she come today of all days,
without her man to share the dance?

Then the usher parted the ballroom doors
and a humble cheerful man slipped inside
barely heeding the familiar lyric,

   "Not for a year, but ever and a day..."

Clarrie searched the room and found her
as he knew he would
then crossed to offer a hand
in invitation to the dance.
Betty rose to accept
and they eased across the floor
while saxes crooned over bass and brushes –
her head pressed gently on his shoulder
where it will always remain.

   *"The Rockies may crumble, Gibralter may tumble,
they're only made of clay..."*

The usher lingered for a moment
to celebrate their golden song
then drifted off in a cloud
to return to his station
at the portal to forever.

Monet's Harbor Sunrise

A small skiff drifted in the harbor
guided by the lazy oars of a fisherman
standing in the hull to better view
the orange circle's reflection
dancing on the gentle waves
in the morning mist.

Monet had to name it something
so he called it what it was:

    "Impression, soleil levant."

A critic, wanting poison for his pen,
seized Monet's title to squeeze
a lethal dose into the radical veins
of the artist and his fellows of the gallery

    (Renoir, Pissarro, Cezanne).

With scathing indignation
he dubbed the lot of them,

    "Mere Impressionists."

The label endures (minus one word)
but how many recall or care to know
the righteous critic's name?

Summer Day on the Current

for Robin on our 22nd anniversary

The placid Current River ever growing
    brightly shimmers in the mid-day sun,
its azure waters cool and southward flowing.

Buried caverns through the limestone bring
    fresh fountains pouring cold ablution
into the placid Current ever growing.

Around the bend another rushing spring
    bursts forth to lend aquatic motion
to the crystal water's southward flowing.

Cheerful floaters revel, tanned and smiling,
    celebrating pleasant summer fun
upon the tranquil waters ever growing.

Gentle breezes set the leaves to rustling
    while time stands still for everyone
along the peaceful river calmly flowing.

Shaded skies foretell the day's conclusion
    and a stellar fantasy has now begun
to dance above the moonlit river glowing:
    its azure waters cool and southward flowing.

Garden of Glass

honoring the glass artistry of Dale Chihuly

A rainbow of serrated globes,
Friends to the water lilies,
Floats in a sculptured pool.

A surreal yellow glass Medusa
Woven through a white crescent trellis
Gleams in the midday sun.

Choirs of chrysanthemums
Sing with multicolored flora
Blown from molten soda, lime and sand.

Sheltered in a geodesic tropics
Orange herons stand on legs of glass
Amid living palms, bamboo and wild orchids.
Towering blue spires
Lift skyward out of the soil
While butterflies dance
In the misty veil of a waterfall.

Nature and the shimmering world within
Happily converge in the florid vision
Of an effervescent man with a patched eye -
A man called Chihuly.

That Dark November Day

The bittersweet harmonies of
Barber's song of ruing
carry me back two score years
to that day I sat intent on the bench -
Barber's accompaniment on the stand.

Ben Walker exploded into the room
"Have you heard about the president? "
My blankness answered,
"Kennedy's been shot! "
My stiffened fingers lifted from the keys.
Dread-filled I stammered,
"Will he be all right? "
Unable to utter the words,
Ben shook his head.

Scenes flicker on our mindscreens
like scratched newsreels -
tears staining Bernstein's face,
Eroica and Resurrection
weeping our televised agony,
Oswald doubled over Ruby's bullets,
a toddler's unbearable salute.

Watching motorcade frames
repeat in slow motion,
we careen on rubber legs:
a nation's heart shattered in Dallas
The somber song plays on:
Housemans's words
Joined with Barber's melodies:

'With Rue my heart is laden."

Borrowed Love Lyric(s)

for sister, Marcia and brother, Jim

What Kind of Fool
Am I, Blue Christmas?
A Fool for Love - That's All.

You Are Love -

The Song is You Belong to
Me and my Shadow.

So What(s)
The Use of Wonderin' (If)
What I Did For Love
Is Sweeping the Country?

Be My (Endless) Love
Is a Many Splendored Thing!

Be My Love
Till the End of Time.

Jerry Singing at his Lathe

Slim and mustached
Jerry sang his heart out
in overalls at his lathe –
the Pavarotti of Kent-Moore Tools.

Curled metal gathered at his feet
as he cut hard steel into usable parts.
He glanced at the prints,
reset the turret to take a second pass
and belted out another chorus.

Jerry retro-dreamed of New York,
of lessons, certificates, Juilliard
and arias finished with outstretched arms –
visions derailed but unforgotten.

Global madness sent him to France.
With a pack and an M1 in place of scores.
Jerry helped set Paris free
yet never left a song on its stages.

Kent-Moore paid him well
and masked by din of colliding metal
Jerry sang and sang and sang all day
for rivet guns and turret lathes.
His voice would melt your heart.

Black Diamonds

In memoriam Asher and Franklin

Farmers flocked to Blossburg's mines
    willing their abandoned plows
    to perpetual dust and rain.

Burrowing into the Tioga hills
    with Keagle picks and sledges,
    they filled their trams with rough cut coal.

Black diamonds - carved for waiting boilers
    of New England mills and trains
    and Pennsylvania's winter stoves.

Brothers, Frank and Asher swung their picks
    in tunnels deep beneath the hills
    and brushed away the clouds of soot.

Their coughs at first seemed harmless
    enough as from nagging colds or flus -
    but deepened as their lungs turned black.

Pain and choking drove them to their beds
    where no medic's art could aid them.
    Then the coroner came to seal their eyes.

A stonecutter's chisel marks their brevity
    on an marble graveyard obelisk
    that pays no homage to their sacrifice.

Nightfall

It's that time again.

The sun pales in the west.
What is there about the dusk
That lowers our songs to sotto voce
We marvel at the fire in the western sky
Yet hear a soft chant of mourning in our souls.

Who can explain that primal veil of sadness?
Could it be the passing of revealing light
Or guilt over dreams left un-chased?
Perhaps we fear Apollo's chariot
Will be lost on the other side.

The sun will greet the new day
And bathe us in all cleansing light
Chance and skill again will dance for us
And what passes will mock our expectations.
What bold psychic can unlock the codes of chaos?

When in the sun's great circling the dusk returns,
To shroud our hearts with curious regrets,
We will take solace in the setting sun
The night will sort the chaos out
And give us needed synthesis.

It's that time again.

Made in the USA
Columbia, SC
12 February 2023

12266385R00067